AmericanGirl Library®

The Babysitter's Handbook

The Care and Keeping of Kids

By Harriet Brown
Illustrated by Stephanie Roth

AmericanGirl®

Published by
Pleasant Company Publications
Copyright © 1999 by
Pleasant Company

Visit our Web site at **americangirl.com**

Printed in China.
03 04 05 06 07 C&C 10 9

American Girl® and American Girl
Library® are registered trademarks of
Pleasant Company.

Editorial Development:
Trula Magruder, Michelle Watkins
Art Direction: Kym Abrams
Managing Art Direction: Ingrid Hess
Design: Donna Beuscher

A special thanks to Molly Kelly,
American Red Cross, Badger Chapter

Questions or comments?
Call 1-800-845-0005 or write to:
American Girl, 8400 Fairway Place,
Middleton, WI 53562.

Library of Congress Cataloging-in-
Publication Data
Brown, Harriet. The babysitter's handbook : the care and keeping of kids /
by Harriet N. Brown ; illustrated by
Stephanie Roth.
p. cm. "American girl library."
Summary: Offers practical advice for
babysitters, covering such basic topics
as feeding, crying, keeping children
amused, first aid, bedtime, and more.
ISBN 1-56247-751-X
1. Babysitting—Handbooks, manuals,
etc.—Juvenile literature.
2. Babysitters—Handbooks, manuals,
etc.—Juvenile literature.
[1. Babysitting—Handbooks, manuals,
etc.] I. Roth, Stephanie, ill. II. American
girl (Middleton, Wis.) III. Title.
HQ769.5.B76 1999
649'.1'0248—dc21 99-13916 CIP

An important note to girls and parents:

The Babysitter's Handbook is designed to provide top-notch tips for caring for kids. What do you do when a child won't stop crying? How can you win over a shy six-year-old? What are the best games to play with babies? How do you handle a tantrum that goes on . . . and on . . . and on?

This handbook has the answers to these questions and much, much more—including tips and tricks from experienced babysitters.

But reading this book will *not* make you a certified babysitter. Books can't take the place of hands-on training—and books can't teach you all you need to know about first aid and CPR. If you take this book on the job, the chapter on first aid will remind you what to do in an emergency—but it will not replace a first-aid class. To be certified, you must take a babysitter training course, like the one offered by the American Red Cross.

You need knowledge to care for kids. So before bounding into the business of caring for kids, find out about babysitter training in your town, and sign up! Taking a course and reading books like this one will get you started. Before long, you'll have the confidence to tell your clients, "I am the best babysitter—ever!"

Your friends at American Girl

Contents

Whether you're a brand-new babysitter or an old pro, these questions and answers will give your skills and confidence a boost!

Babysitter Basics

What's the difference between a mother's helper and a babysitter?

A *mother's helper* entertains kids while the parents are at home—for instance, she might be inside with a child while a parent works in the garden. If a problem comes up, she can ask a parent for help. A *babysitter* cares for kids without an adult around. Since she has more responsibility, she gets paid more. Many sitters start out as mother's helpers because it's great practice.

How do I know if I'm ready to babysit?

There's no hard-and-fast rule. Some girls start to babysit when they're 14. Others start at 11. If you're not sure, ask yourself these questions: Do I feel responsible enough to care for kids? Can I handle discipline problems? Have I taken a Red Cross baby-sitting course? If you answered yes to these questions, you're ready to give babysitting a try.

I've never run a business before. How do I start?

Spread the word! Make flyers and hand them out to your parents' friends. If you have friends who babysit, let them know you're available. They may recommend you for jobs they're not free to take. Once you have a few customers, they'll spread the word for you.

Before you take any job, discuss it with your parents. Make sure they know the family you'll be sitting for. Remember to write down the time the job starts and the address, even if you think you'll remember.

How much should I charge?

Most girls charge $2 to $5 an hour, depending on the number and ages of the children they're sitting. Find out the going rate in your area. Ask friends what they charge. Ask neighbors what they  pay. Some girls will take any pay a client offers. But it's best—for you and for your clients—if you set a fair price and tell the customer what you charge *before* you take the job.

Super Sitter Secret

A big plus

"I took a Red Cross babysitting course in my town. I recommend it for girls who want to be good babysitters. Plus, parents will be more apt to trust you with their kids if they know you're certified!"

Emily
Oregon

American Red Cross

This recognizes
Emily Brown
has completed the
requirements for
Babysitters Training

What if I change my mind?

How would you feel if you were set to do something fun and someone said you couldn't? That's how parents feel when you cancel. If you're sick or a family emergency comes up, clients will understand. But if a friend calls you with ice show tickets on the day before a job, swallow hard and tell her you've made other plans. Your customers are counting on you.

How do I get there—and back home?

When you accept a job outside your neighborhood, let your clients know you'll need transportation. They'll get you there and back. If it's nighttime, make sure a grown-up walks or drives you home. But use your judgment. If for any reason at all you're nervous about someone taking you home, call your parents to come and get you.

What if I don't want to babysit?

If you're asked to babysit for kids you don't get along with, say something like, "I just don't think we're a good fit." Also, turn down jobs you don't think you can handle, such as caring for infant twins—especially if you've never babysat an infant.

What do I need to know before the parents leave?

There's no such thing as too many questions—so ask parents *anything* you're not sure about! The first time you babysit, arrive a few minutes early and get the facts you need. The cards provided in the back of the book are a great place to keep track of client information.

❏ Phone/pager where parents
   can be reached

❏ Address and phone number of house you're in

❏ Time parents expect to be home

❏ Name and phone number of a neighbor

❏ Name and phone number of children's
   doctor and hospital

❏ Nearest intersection of house where you're sitting

❏ Children's food and medicine allergies, if any

❏ What and when to feed children,
   including foods that are off-limits

❏ What to do with dirty diapers and clothes

❏ Bedtime and bedtime rituals for each child

❏ Snacks you can and can't eat

❏ Type of discipline to use if necessary
   (time-outs, no TV, etc.)

❏ Poison control center's number

❏ Emergency number **911**

If I ask a lot of questions, won't the parents think I'm too inexperienced to babysit?

There isn't a question that will seem too dumb to parents. The more questions you ask, the smarter you'll seem. Parents will be thrilled that you know what to ask. After all, you're caring for the most important people in their lives. The more you know, the more confident you and your clients will be that you can handle anything that comes up.

The parents told me to make myself at home. Can I?

A babysitter is not quite a guest and not quite a family member. But you should feel relaxed enough to take care of the children and yourself. If you're hungry, get yourself a snack. But don't make a mess, tie up the phone, or secretly invite friends over—these are just as rude at a client's house as they are at home. And never snoop! How would you feel if someone poked around your room while you were out? Respect a family's privacy the way you'd want others to respect yours.

What if I need help while I'm babysitting?

In a true emergency—for instance, if a child is seriously injured—call 911 and follow the directions given to you. This kind of situation is rare. But if a baby won't stop crying or a toddler locks himself in a room and you don't know what to do, just remember: Stay *calm* so the child will not be frightened. Keep a *cool* head so you can do what you're trained to do. And *call* your parents or the child's parents for help if you need it.

You've arrived on time and met the kids. You've gotten the list of last-minute instructions. Then Mom and Dad wave good-bye and close the door behind them—and the child bursts into tears. Now what?

Everything's O.K.!

Take a deep breath. These tears have nothing to do with you. It's normal for kids—especially little ones five and under—to get upset when their parents leave. These feelings even have a name: *separation anxiety.* With your help, most kids will cheer up pretty quickly once their parents are gone. Here's what you should do:

Reassure them . . .

Remind the child that her parents will be back in a little while. Even though she knows this, she may feel for a minute or two as if her parents will be gone *forever.* Just hearing the words "Don't worry, Mom and Dad will be home later" can help more than you think.

Or hold her hands and clap them together while you sing the words as a silly song: "Mommy goes away and Mommy comes back." It may sound corny to you, but it really does help.

You want kids to trust you, so always tell the truth about when their parents will return. Never promise a toddler that her parents will be back at bedtime if you don't expect them home until much later. If you know her parents will be back late, you could say something like, "When you wake up tomorrow morning, Mom and Dad will be right here at home."

. . . then distract them!

Some babysitters bring little treats for just this moment—a stick of gum for an older child, a colorful Band Aid for a toddler. Other babysitters plan a special activity. These treats and games don't have to be fancy. They just have to help kids get over the "hump" of saying good-bye.

Offer a hug.

Settle the child into your lap with a favorite book.

Put on music and dance around together.

Offer a small treat, like a cookie.

Ask the child to show you her room.

Ask to see her toys.

Pull out a clean sock or pot holder to use as a puppet.

Ask about her pets.

Put on a video.

Pull out a pack of crayons and color.

If it's O.K. with the parents, take the child for a walk.

Say, "Whatever you do, don't smile!"

15

When the crying just won't stop . . .

You've tried every distraction you can think of and the child is still crying. Take a deep breath and stay calm. If a child is crying because his parents have just left, say something like, "Your mommy loves you very much. She and your dad are going to the movies. I know they'll miss you." It doesn't matter *what* you say—what you're really telling the child is that it's O.K. to feel sad for a while. He'll let you know when he's ready for fun.

But what if the crying *never* stops? If you've checked the diaper, tried to feed and soothe the child, and the crying continues, then it's time to get help. Babies and toddlers can't tell you what's wrong. They can't tell you if they're sick or in pain. So before you break into tears yourself, call your parents or the child's parents. They'll want to know what's going on. No one will get angry. Sometimes asking for help is the only thing you *can* do.

Mealtime Do's

Whether serving a snack or dinner, follow these basic rules to make mealtime a safe time.

 **Do** make sure kids are safely occupied while you're preparing the meal.

Do check the temperature of the formula or milk. Shake a drop or two onto your wrist. If it feels hot to you, it's too hot for the baby.

 Do have kids sit down at the table to eat.

Do feed kids only what parents have said is O.K.

Do cut food into small pieces. Round-shaped foods, like hot dogs and grapes, should be cut into half-circles so kids won't choke on them.

and Don'ts

Don't serve food that is too hot to eat. Make sure it has cooled off before you put it on the table.

 Don't leave leftovers out. Put them away in the fridge.

Don't walk away from a child eating—especially a baby. She can wriggle out of her chair and fall.

 Don't serve drinks in fragile glasses. Use plastic cups instead.

Don't leave dirty dishes on the table. Stack them in the sink.

I'm hungry

19

Fun Food

Children can be picky eaters—remember when *you* wouldn't eat anything round or green? Your job is to serve them healthy snacks, not to fill them up with junk food. The key to feeding kids healthy food and keeping them happy is to make mealtime fun. Sound impossible? Try these tasty treats!

Bagel faces

Spread cream cheese over half a bagel. Use vegetable or fruit pieces to make hair, eyes, and a smile.

Cinnamon-sugar toast

Butter a slice of toast. Sprinkle a mixture of cinnamon and sugar over it. Cut off the crusts.

Sandwich shapes

Use cookie cutters to turn plain old PB and J into hearts, stars, and other dazzling designs!

Cracker sandwiches

Make cracker sandwiches with peanut butter, jelly, cream cheese, tuna salad, or sliced turkey.

Peewee pizzas

Spread tomato sauce onto an English muffin. Add cubes of cheese. Microwave on HIGH until the cheese melts. Let the child make a pizza face with cut vegetables.

Ants on a log

Spread peanut butter on a celery stick. Add a line of raisins.

Silly Servings

Sometimes *what* you feed kids isn't as important as *how* you feed them. A giggle or two can make everything taste better!

Have an indoor picnic

Spread a tablecloth or old sheet on the floor. Pack simple picnic food in lunch boxes or in a picnic basket. Pour juice or milk from a thermos.

Switcheroo

Let kids pretend they're the babysitters and you're the kid. Ask them to serve you—and themselves—a premade snack.

Play restaurant

Pretend the kids have come to a restaurant. You're the waitress (and cook!). Tell them "today's special." Write their orders on a notepad. While you're preparing the meal, give them paper and crayons. Let them know they have to "pay" for the meal with their artwork!

Super Sitter Secret

Smooth sailing

"I like to make happy faces on sandwiches with raisins for the eyes and mouth. Or I stick a straw in the sandwich and tape on a paper sail for a sandwich boat!"

Robin
Vermont

I'm hungry.

Cleanup Time!

If there's one thing parents dislike, it's coming home to a messy kitchen. So make sure you clean up after yourself and the children. You don't have to wash every dish, but tidy up the kitchen the best you can. If you're caring for an infant, you may not have time to clean. That's O.K. Even grown-ups let chores slide when they're taking care of a baby!

Most kids enjoy helping with cleanup. Make up a silly song like "Clean up, clean up, everybody clean up!" or "Kristy is a helper, a helper, a helper. Kristy is a helper, yes she is." Choose chores that are right for each age. Toddlers and preschoolers can dry silverware and put it away. School-age kids can load the dishwasher or wash dishes. If you're not sure where something goes, ask. Kids love knowing more than you do.

Your Turn

I'm hungry!

You forgot to eat before you came to babysit, and now you're starving. What should you do?

No one wants you to starve. Help yourself to a small snack: cheese and crackers, a peanut butter sandwich, cookies and milk. But don't open foil-wrapped packages or dig through the freezer. Parents won't appreciate it if you eat tomorrow night's dinner!

Want to be everyone's favorite babysitter? Just remember these three little words: play with kids. *What kids want most is your attention. Chances are, the kids you're babysitting will love anything you suggest—as long as you do it together.*

Baby Play

Little ones need simple games. Be prepared to play them over and over!

Where's the ball?

Sit opposite baby on the floor. Gently roll a small ball toward her. Say something like, "Where's the ball? There it is! Can you roll it back to me?"

Which hand?

Put a small toy in one hand. Put both hands behind your back and ask baby to point to the hand that has the toy.

Want to sing?

Don't forget all those songs you learned as a child. Try singing them "Itsy-Bitsy Spider," "I'm a Little Teapot," and "Head-Shoulders-Knees-and-Toes." And remember: It's all new to them!

Look what I see!

Carry baby around the room, pointing out interesting objects—a vase of flowers, a ticking clock. Let her look out the window, and talk to her about what's outside: "Look, there's a tree with green leaves."

Where's the baby?

Pretend you can't find the baby. Look behind chairs, in closets, etc., saying things like, "Where's Sadie? I can't find Sadie!" Then whirl around, point to her, and say, *"There* she is!"

See the animal?

Place stuffed animals throughout the house. Now walk baby through the house, pointing out and naming every animal you see: "Look, there's a bunny! I see a penguin. Do you see the kitty cat?"

Dance with me!

Put on some music and get moving! Babies love it when you spin them around. Don't do it right after a meal, and stop if you get dizzy.

Super Sitter Secrets

Dress the part

"Don't wear necklaces or dangling earrings. Babies love to pull on them, and you could end up with sore ears or a broken necklace. Wear nice but comfortable clothes. You'll look professional and still be able to crawl around with the kids."

Melissa
Indiana

Justina
Arkansas

Toddler Time

Toddlers think everything's funny. The best games and activities for them are short and silly!

Dances with scarves

Bring out a handful of colorful scarves, turn on the music, and dance. Show toddlers how to wave scarves in time to the music.

Hide-and-seek

A toddler will hide in the same place over and over, so act surprised each time you find her. Make sure you always know where she is.

Creative coloring

Make a one-of-a-kind coloring book. Fold three sheets of construction paper in half. Staple them together in the shape of a book. Draw pictures of the child, her parents, and her pets. Ask her to color them in.

Planet Purr

Pretend the sofa is a spaceship. With the child in your lap, lean left and right as the ship zooms into space. Once you "land," climb off onto Planet Purr, where everyone becomes a kitty! Get onto the ship to become human again.

Color clues

Toddlers love to be right—
especially when you're wrong!
Sing, "Libby is a big girl, a big girl,
a big girl. Libby is a big girl, and
her shirt is blue!" Be sure to say
the wrong color. The first few times
you might have to correct yourself:
"Blue? Noooooo, it's pink!" Soon
she'll be correcting you!

Peewee pet care

For this emergency, you'll need
a toy truck or car, strips of cloth,
and a few stuffed animals. Ask the
toddler to bandage the "injured"
animals and transport them in the
ambulance. Don't forget the siren!

Change machine

Drape a sheet over a table. Every
time a child goes through the
"change machine," she becomes
something new—firefighter, frisky
puppy, or ballerina!

Ruff!

Around town

Turn cardboard boxes into a town. Get out toy cars
and as many "people" as you can find.

Kid Games

Older kids have their own ideas of how to have fun. Offer these when they're ready for something new.

Basketball

Crumple pieces of newspaper to make ten balls for each kid. Set out a trash can. Each child tries to make as many baskets as possible.

Letter writing

Ask kids to "send" you letters, describing what they want to do the next time you babysit. Let them seal the letters in envelopes and drop them into a "mailbox" or "mailbag" you've set out. Read them when you get home!

Card games

Bring a deck of playing cards, and show kids a new game each time you babysit. In Concentration, lay out all the cards facedown. Take turns flipping over two cards. If the numbers match, pick up the cards and take another turn. At the end, the person with the most cards wins!

Magazine scavenger hunt

Give each kid an old magazine or catalog, along with a list of things to find, cut out, and glue onto a piece of paper.

Soft volleyball

Run a piece of string across the floor, and have kids stand on either side. Blow up a balloon. Toss it back and forth without letting it touch the ground. You can play while on your knees!

Junior babysitter

Kids love coming up with games for the little ones. Put them in charge of creating activities for toddlers or babies. Be sure to play the games with them!

Super Sitter Secret

Clean queen

"One time I was babysitting four little girls. They were bored, and the house was a mess. So I invented a game. In each room, a girl was the queen and the rest of us were servants. She told us what to pick up or clean. We appointed a new queen for each room. It worked like a charm, and their mom was happy about the house!"

Anna
Washington

Wanna play?

Pack Up!

Kids will get a kick out of anything you bring along. Your goodies don't have to be new—they'll be new to the kids, and that's all that matters.

- ❑ Scarves

- ❑ Children's video or music tape

- ❑ Kids' scissors

- ❑ Colorful Band-Aids

- ❑ Face paints

- ❑ Small toys (truck, doll, etc.)

- ❑ Small jigsaw puzzle

- ❑ Stuffed animal

- ❑ Old sock or pot holder for a puppet

- ❑ Bubbles

- ❑ Small ball

- ❑ Stickers

- ❑ Elmer's glue or a glue stick

- ❑ Board game

- ❑ Playing cards

- ❑ Children's books

- ❑ Old catalogs or magazines

- ❑ Night-light

- ❑ Paper and envelopes

- ❑ Coloring books and crayons

- ❑ Temporary tattoos

- ❑ Paintbrush and paints

Uh-oh. The kids have been arguing—and arguing—all evening. You feel more like a referee than a babysitter! How can you stop the squabbling?

Cool Them Off

First, make sure the kids don't hurt each other, and give everyone a little time to settle down. Put the children in different rooms, or in opposite corners of the same room. Tell them, "We're all going to take a time-out for five minutes." Set a timer, and make sure everybody's quiet until it rings.

Talk it out

Many arguments aren't about anything important—they're the way kids let off steam at one another. But when real conflicts do come up, it's your job to help sort things out.

The best way to do that is to have the kids talk to each other. Stand one on either side of you, facing each other. Give each child two minutes to express her feelings, one at a time. A few important rules: The kids must talk to each other, not to you. They must talk about their own feelings, not just rehash what the other one said or did. And they must really listen to what the other child says.

Once both kids have aired their feelings, the argument may be over. But if the kids are still fighting, you have to help them work it out. Ask each of them to offer a fair solution to the problem. If they can't come up with a plan they both like, offer a compromise. If the argument is over a doll, for instance, you might suggest that each child take a five-minute turn with the doll. Or point out another doll that could be added to the game.

If the kids just can't agree, let them know that you will solve the problem your way—by taking away the toy or ending the game. Give them one more chance to work it out, and then do what you said you would.

Super Sitter Secret

Funny face

"When kids are fighting, I set them on chairs across from each other and tell them to give each other ugly faces. Before you know it, they can't frown, and they end up laughing!"

Jen
Wisconsin

She hit me!

I'm Telling!

Kids tell on each other for two reasons.

They can't solve the problem

Help them talk to each other to try to resolve the problem themselves. If they can't, *you* make a decision—and make sure everyone sticks to it.

They want your attention

Don't watch TV. Play with the kids. If they don't want you to play, stay close enough to hear what's going on. Make sure they know you're around. They'll be glad, even if they don't seem to care.

If they're still tattling, say, "I won't listen to tattling, but I *will* listen if you want to tell me how *you* feel or about something *you* did."

Super Sitter Secret

A happy medium

"While I was babysitting, one kid wanted to watch *Little Women* and the other wanted to watch *Toy Story*. I asked them to decide on their own, then went to fix popcorn. When I came back, the kids had agreed to *Little Women* because they had seen *Toy Story* once already."

Carly
Wisconsin

Babies and toddlers can't say "I'm scared" in words. Instead, they tell you with tears. To comfort little ones who are frightened or upset, try the following ideas.

Little Kids

Talk

Babies may not understand *what* you say, but they react to the *way* you say it. Talk to them in a low, soothing voice, and keep talking even if you run out of things to say. For instance: "There, there, baby, everything's O.K., you're O.K., everyone loves you, you're going to be fine, you'll see, it's O.K."

Walk

Movement helps calm kids. Pick up a baby or toddler and walk her around the room or house.

Touch

Start with a hug. Move on to patting or rubbing the baby's back, bottom, or chest. Find a steady rhythm she likes, and rub or pat firmly (but not hard enough to hurt).

Distract

Once the baby starts to calm down, distract her with a toy, a book, a peek out the window, or anything else that catches her interest.

Use body language

Long before they learn to talk, kids communicate with body language. You can use this special language to comfort children. Kneel beside the child so you can look into her eyes. Smile. Tilt your head to one side. After you do this a few times, it will feel natural. Try it—it works!

Super Sitter Secret

Travel light

"I *always* bring a night-light in my backpack when I go babysitting. Some kids are very afraid of the dark!"

Joan
Rhode Island

Three and Up

Kids this age can usually tell you exactly what's scaring them. That helps! Once you know what's frightening them, you can do something about it. Here are some of the most common fears children have.

The dark

Don't flip off the lights and race to a lit room yourself. This can make kids nervous about the dark. Dim the lights or put on a night-light. Then let them see that you're not afraid. Sit on the bed and tell them a story. Or give them a favorite stuffed animal or doll. Say, "Put your baby to sleep." This puts them in charge of their fear.

Stormy weather

You'll find out about this fear only if a thunderstorm actually happens while you're babysitting. Stay with the child. Turn on a light even if he's already gone to bed. Talk to him about what a thunderstorm really is, in words he can understand: "Thunder is the noise we hear when two big rain clouds bump into each other up in the sky. Isn't that silly?" Hug him, play with him, sing songs, tell funny stories, or do anything else that takes his mind off the storm outside.

Scary thoughts or dreams

Tell the child to imagine that his mind is a television and he's holding the remote control. Have him imagine that he's clicking the remote and changing the channel from a scary show to a silly one. Sit with him until he's asleep.

Your Turn

Night noises

You just finished watching a scary movie on TV, and now you hear strange noises in the house. What do you do when *you're* scared?

The best cure for this kind of fear is prevention: don't watch scary movies or read scary books—especially while you're babysitting. If you do get nervous, check the house to reassure yourself that everything's secure. Call a parent or a neighbor. If you're truly convinced you hear an intruder, call 911. It's better to be safe than sorry.

Mash the monsters!

No matter how often you reassure them, some kids will still be afraid of things that go bump in the night. If this happens, get creative. Here's what other girls have done to move the monsters out.

"I bring a spray bottle filled with water. At bedtime, I tell the kids it's monster spray and spray it around the room. Then I tuck it back in my pack, and they feel safe!"

Channing
Kansas

"The four-year-old that I watch is afraid of the dark. So we surround the bed with his stuffed animals. We call them Super Toys. They keep out bogeymen and ghosts."

Laura
Maryland

"If the kids say there's a monster under their bed, I put a carrot into a sack and slip it under the bed. I tell them monsters love carrots, and they shrink to fit inside the bag. After a few minutes I grab the bag, rush outside, and put it into the garbage can. They always fall asleep right after that!"

Kelly
California

The kids you're babysitting insist they always *have candy with dinner. You know that's not true—but what do you do?*

You're in Charge

Kids can be surprisingly persuasive when they want you to do things their way. Try these wise words the next time you don't know what to say.

Offer a substitute
She says: "My parents make me hot chocolate every night—and they let me drink it in bed."

You say: "Hot chocolate in bed isn't a good idea. I'll give you a glass of milk and read you a story while you drink it in the kitchen."

Offer a substitute that you feel good about. Ask parents about the rules when they get home so that next time you'll know.

Give her a choice
She says: "I just want to jump from the table onto the sofa *one* time."

You say: "You have a choice. You can either climb down from the table yourself, or I can help you down. Which do you choose?"

When you give children a choice, you're teaching them that you make the rules but that they have some control over what happens.

Think about safety

He says: "Don't tell my parents! I'll never ride my bike without my helmet again, I promise!"

You say: "I do have to tell your parents—not to be mean, but because I know they care about you. When it comes to your safety, they have to know exactly what happened."

When the parents return, let them know what the child has done. Remember: your job is to keep kids safe, even if it makes you unpopular.

Enforce the rules—calmly

She says: "I won't get ready for bed! I hate you! I wish you would go away and never come back!"

You say (calmly): "I'm sorry you feel that way. But you still have to brush your teeth."

Sometimes kids say mean things to see how you'll react, but they'll usually calm down and do what you ask. If you feel a child really doesn't like you, let her parents know. Say, "I'm sorry, but Megan and I aren't a good fit." They'll understand.

Make an agreement

He says: "I'm not cleaning up my toys, and you can't make me!"

You say: "I can't make you, and I'm not going to try. But if you don't clean up, I won't have time to read you a story because I'll be too busy cleaning up toys. And I will have to tell your parents what happened."

Show the child that his behavior has consequences. And if you do decide to take away a story or a treat, don't back down.

Stay calm

She says: "I'm not going to bed! No, no, no, no, no!"

You say: Nothing. You don't want to keep the tantrum going. Stay near her, but let her cry. She will eventually calm down.

Sometimes silence works best. Kids try tantrums to see if they'll get what they want. If tantrums work, they'll keep throwing them—which is not good for anybody.

Super Sitter Secret

You're the boss

"Even though you may not feel like it, you *are* in charge. The kids look up to you!"

Heather
Connecticut

Never changed a diaper before? Don't panic—it's easier than you think!

Get Ready!

Stock supplies

Get supplies ready before you lay the baby down on the changing table: baby wipes, clean diapers, and any cream or ointment the parents have asked you to apply. Make sure supplies are out of the way so she can't kick them off. Also, be sure there's a garbage can or diaper pail nearby for disposing of used diapers.

Remove her clothes

When removing the baby's pants, always keep a hand on her so she doesn't fall off the table. If her clothes are dirty, put clean ones on after you've changed the diaper.

Distract her

Babies love to look at things that move. Many families hang mobiles over the changing area. Blow on the mobile or tap it right before you get to work. You might also talk, sing, or make faces at the baby.

Be gentle

To avoid bumping the baby's head, keep one hand under the back of her head as you lay her down.

Keep her busy

Give the baby something to hold or chew during a diaper change so her hands don't get in your way. If no toys are handy, offer a clean diaper or washcloth.

Diaper Demo

Once everything's prepared, you're ready to change the diaper. Follow these step-by-step instructions, and changing a diaper will be a snap!

1. Undo diaper. Gently grasp baby's ankles and lift. Slide diaper from under baby's bottom. Fold edges so nothing falls out.

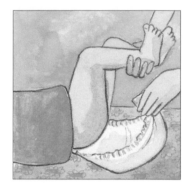

2. Set baby's bottom down gently. Dispose of used diaper, but keep a hand on baby at all times. Even a newborn can roll off a changing table.

3. Carefully wipe baby's bottom from front to back with a baby wipe. For boys, lay a clean diaper over the penis to avoid surprising showers.

4. Apply lotion if parents have asked you to. Then gently grasp baby's feet and lift. Slide a clean diaper under baby's bottom and fasten the tabs from back to front.

5. Dress the baby in clean clothes. Then set her someplace safe—in a crib or on the carpet where you can see her—while you wash your hands.

Poop.

Super Sitter Secret

Bathroom break

"If you have to go to the bathroom while watching a baby, put her in a crib or a playpen while you're gone. Never leave her out. I learned that the hard way. After just two minutes, the baby made a mess—and she could have gotten hurt."

Andi
Florida

Potty Plan

Most kids begin toilet training between ages two and three. And every child goes through the process differently. To help them do their best, try these tips:

❑ When a child says she has to go potty, she means *right now!* So don't say, "Wait a minute." Stop what you're doing and take her to the bathroom.

❑ Never scold a child who goes to the bathroom in his pants. If he doesn't make it to the toilet, praise him for trying, and help him into clean clothes. When he does go potty on the toilet, always praise him.

❑ Boys may sit down to pee—it's neater that way. If they want to stand, help aim their bodies so they're peeing into the toilet.

❑ Kids under five may need help cleaning up after pooping. Ask them to stand and lean over. This makes your job easier. Remember to wipe front to back.

❑ Two- and three-year-olds often forget to go to the bathroom. Every so often, ask them, "Do you need to go potty?" But don't force the issue.

❑ Make sure the child washes before she leaves the bathroom. Slip soap into her hands and turn on warm water. Remember to wash your hands, too, especially after changing diapers.

Stop accidents before *they happen.*

Safety First

Check for potential hazards

Watch out for possible dangers like matches, electrical cords, plastic bags, cleaners, medicines, tools, and even clutter. Use childproof locks and childproof sockets if they're available, and keep bathroom doors closed.

Never tell strangers you're alone.

Make sure the child can't pull anything off a high area onto herself.

Keep rugs flat so kids won't trip over them.

Don't leave the house

As soon as parents leave, lock all doors. If someone knocks on a door, don't open it. Say, "Mr. Smith can't come to the door, but he asked me to take a message." If someone calls, don't tell the caller you're alone. Say, "I'm sorry, Ms. Smith isn't available right now. Can I take a message?"

Know your job site

Ask parents where they keep the first-aid kit, flashlight, and fire extinguisher. Ask how to work the alarm system, the smoke detector, and any equipment you'll be allowed to use, such as the VCR, TV, or microwave.

Know where the emergency equipment is kept.

Keep plants out of reach.

Keep all cabinets shut.

Never leave knives out.

Face pot handles toward the back of the stove.

Owl

Always keep an eye on children

In the blink of an eye, babies can stuff tiny objects into their mouths. Toddlers can slip into pools, tubs, or toilets. Older kids can disappear around a corner. So keep your eyes on kids at all times. Continue to check on them even after they go to bed.

53

Be Prepared

Emergencies are less scary when you know what to do. Being prepared will help you to stay calm. Take the Babysitter's Training Course offered by the American Red Cross, or Safe Sitter classes held at a hospital in your community.

No matter how minor a child's injury—from a bee sting to a nosebleed—call the parents. That doesn't mean always call parents immediately. In some cases, you'll need to call 911 or the poison control center, or help the child yourself, before you call anyone. Once the child is out of danger, then inform the parents.

When working around blood, *always* wear rubber gloves. First-aid kits should have gloves, but buy a pair and keep them in your babysitter's bag, just in case.

This is not a first-aid book. Nothing replaces hands-on first-aid training. But the following basic tips will help guide you through emergencies.

Insect stings and bites

If you see a stinger, scrape it off with something stiff, like a credit card or playing card. Wash bites and stings with soap and water. Wrap an ice cube in a paper towel and hold it to a sting to reduce swelling.

Cuts and scrapes

Small cuts and scrapes can bleed quite a bit. Use a clean washcloth to press lightly on the injury until the bleeding stops. Then gently wash the cut with soap and water. Apply a Band-Aid— even if you don't think one is needed. It will make the child feel better.

Nosebleeds

Tilt the child's head forward. Pinch the bottom of the nose closed to stop the bleeding. Never tilt the head backward.

Fever

If a child feels warm to the touch, call the parents. In the meantime, encourage the child to rest and offer her water or juice to drink.

Heavy bleeding

For a wound that spurts or gushes, *call 911 immediately.* If someone else is in the area, ask that person to call 911. Then press a clean cloth firmly against the wound and raise it higher than the heart. Keep pressing for at least five minutes. When the bleeding stops, tape the cloth in place and keep the child warm until help arrives.

Super Sitter Secret

Seeing red

"If kids get a small cut, use a red or dark-colored towel so the blood doesn't scare them."

Sarah
Wisconsin

Owl

Choking

If a choking child can't talk, cough, or breathe, you must get rid of the obstruction immediately. *Don't take the time to call 911 unless the child passes out.* (If someone else can call 911 for you, ask him or her to do so.) As soon as you've forced the object out, call 911. Choking is *very* scary. Even after you've taken a first-aid course, continue to practice the steps on a doll so you'll be prepared.

For a child:

1. Stand behind the child. Wrap your arms around her waist, as if you're giving her a hug.

2. Make a fist. Place the thumb side against the child's belly, just above the belly button. Grab the fist with your other hand.

3. Thrust or quickly pull your fist up and into the belly. Repeat until whatever the child is choking on pops out of her mouth and she starts to breathe.

4. Call 911 and then the parents.

For an infant:

1. Sit down. Turn the infant onto his belly. Lay him facedown along your arm. Hold his jaw to support his head. Don't cover his nose or mouth. Keep his head lower than his body.

2. Place the heel of your other hand between the shoulder blades. Give five forceful blows with the heel of your hand.

3. While supporting the head, flip the child over onto his back. Place three fingers over his breastbone, between the nipples.

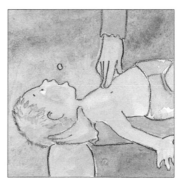

4. Press down firmly on the center of the breastbone five times. Repeat steps 2, 3, and 4 until the object comes out.

5. Call 911 and then the parents.

Ow!

57

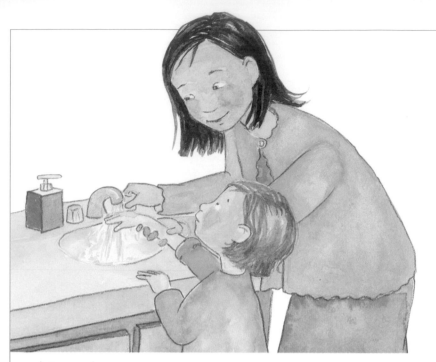

Minor burns

Run cool water over red, unbroken skin for at least five minutes. Don't put on a Band-Aid. Don't apply medicine, butter, or any kind of cream. Don't use ice. Small burns are painful, so reassure the child that she'll be O.K. Call the parents.

For any burn worse than red skin or a small blister, cool with water and *call 911 immediately*—even if you aren't sure how bad the burn is. Then call the parents.

Swallowing nonfood

If a child swallows anything that isn't food, *call the poison control center immediately*. (If you don't have the number, call 911.) Have the bottle nearby when you call. You may be asked to give the child milk or water to drink. You may also be asked to give her a dose of *syrup of ipecac*, which causes vomiting. Most families keep this in the medicine cabinet or first-aid kit. Don't give the child the syrup, milk, or water unless a poison control operator tells you to. Call the parents.

Call 911

If you're faced with any other emergency, *call 911*. The 911 operator may ask for the address and will want to know what kind of emergency is going on. Stay calm, and follow the operator's instructions.

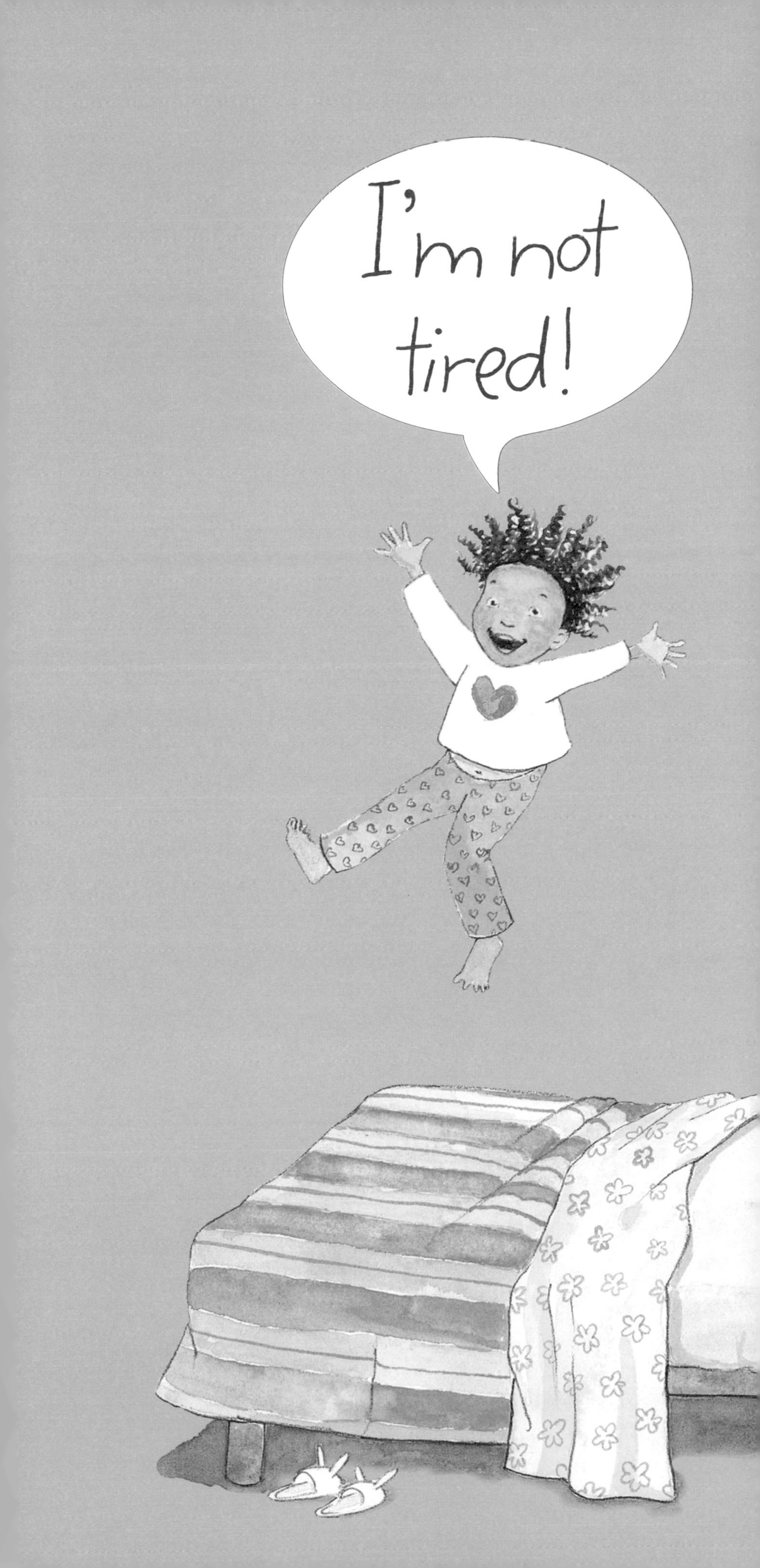
I'm not tired!

How do you turn a bouncing child into a sleeping angel? Read on!

Make a Timetable

Putting children to bed takes time and planning. Allow 30 to 45 minutes for changing into pajamas, brushing teeth, reading books or telling a story, and cuddling. For instance, if the parents have asked you to put the kids to bed at 8:30, start getting them ready no later than 7:45. Babies and toddlers are a whole different story. Ask parents what routines they follow to get their tiny ones to sleep.

Note: Babies under age one should always be put to sleep on their backs to reduce the risk of SIDS (Sudden Infant Death Syndrome).

Give plenty of warning

Kids need help moving from one activity to another. Saying, "It's bedtime *right now!*" is sure to cause tears and tantrums. Instead, say, "In ten minutes we're going to get ready for bed."

Follow routines

Kids often have bedtime routines. Ask parents about these. At what time do the kids slip into their pajamas? Do they need to pick up their toys before bed? Can they have a snack? Should you leave their bedroom light on or turn it off?

Share a story

Stories are a great way to end the day. Slip kids into bed, tuck them in, then read or tell them a story. If the kids want to read to you, let them.

Lights-out!

Stick to the routine, especially the first time you sit for a family. When it's time for lights-out, be firm. Kids will know that you mean what you say—and will be much more likely to listen!

Super Sitter Secret

Sweet dreams

"When I'm babysitting a child who can't read, and I read a story at bedtime, I always end with 'and they went to sleep and lived happily ever after,' even though most books don't say that. It helps the child think about going to sleep as a nice thing instead of dreading it."

Julia
Delaware

I'm not tired!

61

Sleepy-time tips

Many children need help falling asleep, especially babies and toddlers. Here are some tried-and-true ways to help.

Rock or carry an infant. Try different moves—fast, slow, up-and-down jiggling—until you find one that works.

Lay a sleeping baby down s-l-o-w-l-y. Dropping him suddenly into the crib is guaranteed to jolt him awake.

Firmly pat or rub a toddler's back or tummy.* Try a combination of patting and rubbing.
*Read the note on p. 60.

Sing to a child once she's in bed. Lullabies are good, but almost any song will help a child settle down.

Put on a night-light. Or turn on a light in the hall or bathroom and adjust the door until it feels right for the child.

Promise to come back and check on the child in 10 or 15 minutes—and make sure you do.

Your Turn

I'm tired!

The kids are asleep, and you're tired, too. Is it O.K. for you to take a nap on the couch?

Falling asleep on the job is unprofessional, and it could be dangerous. Until the parents return, your job is to be alert and in charge. (A good night's sleep the night before should help.) Splash cold water on your face, jog in place—do whatever you must to stay awake.

Super Sitter Stuff

You know what it takes to care for kids. Now here are some tools to help you run the best business on the block. Use the business cards to spread the word. To stay organized, fill out the family profile and emergency information cards. For more cards, copy these or create your own!

Business cards

Add your personal information to the business cards and pass them out to potential clients. Give them only to people you and your parents know and trust.

Family profile

Before your first job with a client, gather the information requested on the card. Keep all your client cards in an index card box or binder.

Emergency information

Be sure to fill out all the emergency information on the cards. Getting this information is one of the most important parts of your job!

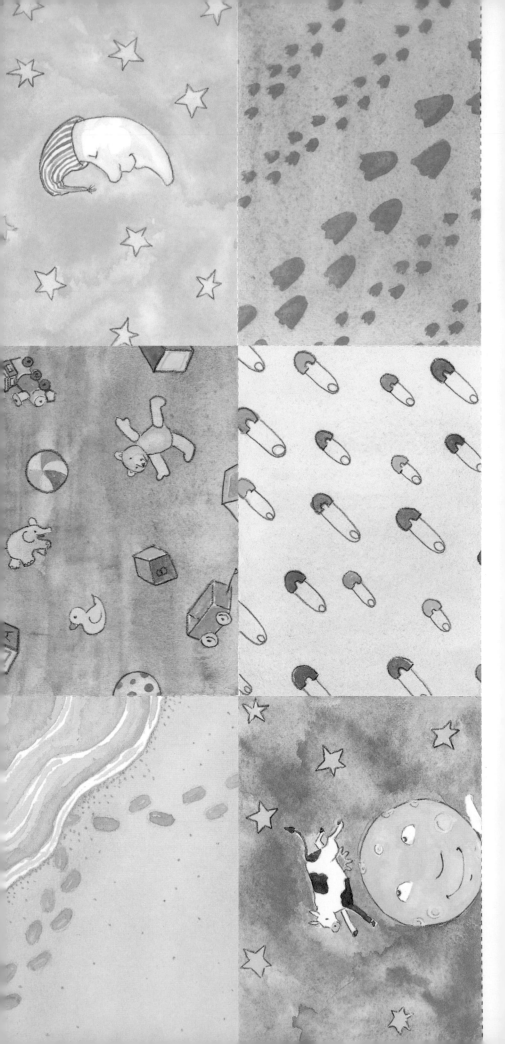

Family Profile Cards

Family Profile

Name of child _____ Age _____ Birthday _____

Name of child _____ Age _____ Birthday _____

Name of child _____ Age _____ Birthday _____

Rate per hour _____ Allergies _____ Bedtimes _____

Favorite games _____ Favorite books _____

Favorite foods _____ Things the kids hate _____

Family Profile

Name of child _____ Age _____ Birthday _____

Name of child _____ Age _____ Birthday _____

Name of child _____ Age _____ Birthday _____

Rate per hour _____ Allergies _____ Bedtimes _____

Favorite games _____ Favorite books _____

Favorite foods _____ Things the kids hate _____

Family Profile

Name of child _____ Age _____ Birthday _____

Name of child _____ Age _____ Birthday _____

Name of child _____ Age _____ Birthday _____

Rate per hour _____ Allergies _____ Bedtimes _____

Favorite games _____ Favorite books _____

Favorite foods _____ Things the kids hate _____

Emergency Information

Parents' names

Address   Nearest intersection

Home phone   Cell phone/pager

Close neighbor's name and phone

Doctor   Preferred hospital

Poison control center number

Emergency Information

Parents' names

Address   Nearest intersection

Home phone   Cell phone/pager

Close neighbor's name and phone

Doctor   Preferred hospital

Poison control center number

Emergency Information

Parents' names

Address   Nearest intersection

Home phone   Cell phone/pager

Close neighbor's name and phone

Doctor   Preferred hospital

Poison control center number

Family Profile Cards

Family Profile

Name of child   Age   Birthday

Name of child   Age   Birthday

Name of child   Age   Birthday

Rate per hour   Allergies   Bedtimes

Favorite games   Favorite books

Favorite foods   Things the kids hate

Family Profile

Name of child   Age   Birthday

Name of child   Age   Birthday

Name of child   Age   Birthday

Rate per hour   Allergies   Bedtimes

Favorite games   Favorite books

Favorite foods   Things the kids hate

Family Profile

Name of child   Age   Birthday

Name of child   Age   Birthday

Name of child   Age   Birthday

Rate per hour   Allergies   Bedtimes

Favorite games   Favorite books

Favorite foods   Things the kids hate

Emergency Information

Parents' names

Address   Nearest intersection

Home phone   Cell phone/pager

Close neighbor's name and phone

Doctor   Preferred hospital

Poison control center number

Emergency Information

Parents' names

Address   Nearest intersection

Home phone   Cell phone/pager

Close neighbor's name and phone

Doctor   Preferred hospital

Poison control center number

Emergency Information

Parents' names

Address   Nearest intersection

Home phone   Cell phone/pager

Close neighbor's name and phone

Doctor   Preferred hospital

Poison control center number